DISPLACEMENT GEOLOGY

Displacement Geology

Tamsin Spencer Smith

fmsbw

San Francisco, California

"Were the Eye Not Sunlike" was published in *Lightning Strikes II: 22 Poets. 22 Artists* (San Francisco, CA: Dolby Chadwick Gallery, 2019); "A Principle of Double Reflection" appeared as a broadside to commemorate the 101st birthday of Lawrence Ferlinghetti (Emeryville, CA: Western Editions, 2020); and "Adagio Cantabile" was published in *STAY INSPIRED: Shelter in Place 2020* (San Francisco, CA: Dolby Chadwick Gallery, 2020).

Cover artwork by Kevin Earl Taylor

Author photo by Matt Gonzalez

fmsbw

San Francisco, California

For Una & for David

CONTENTS

I.

Divergent Boundaries

COLOSSUS

We fell first
Like animals
On the scent
Of sensation

Fleet as the flagship
Species worth saving
Ran pole to equator
& tagged ourselves wild

O forager of the vanishing world,

Our lust has melted
Leaving flood and ruin
To flip channels as
The charismatic beg

In solitary circles
Their bell gable bodies
(once opulent)
Spyhop at solstice

Every 14 days another language falls away

We came for aurora
But stayed for the ice
The jazz of unnatured snowflakes
The jive of human debris

We played for the sunset
Lost hold of the trees
Plucked at our boreal arrows
Blew on our mossy reeds

Pale sister-bird
Song me another please
For the snow goose, the whale shark are calling

BENEDICTION AT THE ACADEMY OF SCIENCES

Moths heretofore mudpuddled
The flooded soil of the Amazon
Gathering protein and nutrient
To fuel flight and love-making

From fossils we may trace their insect antics
As far back as the continental drift
When first these fans of celestial fire
Brushed the cage of human desire

Moths fed the orchids
Charles Darwin once loved
Also spun silk for empress and empire
Pressed into service from Pangea to today

When scientists find
Some have begun
To feast on the tears
Of sleeping birds

Is it for salt or grief
Or like some freed storm
Ruffling a lake surface
To engineer speed

A cloud of *Negeta luminosa*
Assembles overhead
Moths lay shade upon
The living and the dead

OUROBOROS OVERLAPPING

For Walter and Mary Munk

From a sweep of recessed green
Somewhere between crocodile and mangrove
I see those manatee are watching me
Certain the better adjective was bream
But I dream of trailing fins
Cities named for holes
A catalogue of ships
Of human wars
And being fly

For to jump like a devil ray
Conveys the shock of under sides
As the motion of a head
In waves inscribes
Water is orbital
Rolls deeper
The downer
You go

Thin electric wires
Incline to combine
Eels must weep
In angstrom
But leave
No rust

PAPER GLAIVE

For Beau Beausoleil

Cairo writes, Beirut publishes, Bagdad reads
So goes an old Arab saying
I found between browned pages
In the bargain bin at one of two
Remaining book stalls on 24th
A once literary alley though
The tally's no better in North Beach
Beau's closed The Great Overland
& Aardvark's quit the Castro
Still & all as it is with mourning
Mecca is a much-abused term
In our age of unrelenting upgrades
And Earth overshoot days
Yet loss has a way of finding its like
Erasing miles and the clock

From the pitch of a vast denuded expanse
Movement baits the naked eye
To follow without fail
The foreign familiar
The impossible possibility
Letters that form and reform
After a fault is thrown
The blade of a single phrase
In slow lustrate detonation
Louder than today's news
& more cutting

POSTCARD FROM PARADISE

"And yet many living in Kilauea's shadow
welcome the eruption, express reverence for Pele
and thank her — even when the lava destroys their home."
New York Times Magazine, May 21, 2018.

The earth is falling from the sky
Another forced and sudden separation

Madame Pele Goddess of Fire cradles
Her basalt breast beseeching the surge

Diffuse not as olivine and ooze
Cast your fate of effervescent stone

Birthmarked by fault and shadow
Tangled vines of perpetual green

Twilight lithified
& so nearly precious

Humankind must know what's been
Lost beside this black sand isle

Full of forest and legend —

Travelers explore the bones of history
To ignore news from home
Pluck at souvenirs to tuck behind their ears

Laughing as the rain pours down
Red blossom calls to twisted trunk

All is not lost my love
Look for me in peridot
Pele's palest tear

A PRINCIPLE OF DOUBLE REFLECTION

Young man, you've been to school — Who was Telemachus?

Lawrence Ferlinghetti

Boy sails off to learn something from the islands of old kings
Unsure of wayward arrows until the captive face of war
Shows him what she knows of silver tongues and homecoming
One may discern an undertone of adaptation
It is the nature of women to fill white sails
You will measure the angle of stars by line break
Where in his palm five moons bed at the finger base
One hand waxes
Revolution from the left
Each phase a new sea
Jib fills with what the mind casts off
You cannot touch the bottom of this journey
A center must hold itself
Make shelter for the strange
Shape from seaweed alone
A spine a masthead
The greatest beauty in the known world
Whispers through the kindling of a mighty hull
But you have never been afraid of words
Thousands upon thousands launched
Unflagged, unsinkable

GOOD CROSSING

Three rivers add water
To the Euphrates to feed
Centuries of palm, grape, and sugar beet
Heaped with rainfed wheat on burlap sacks
I study the magazine's blown up image to feel
Your laughter fill the market stall
Teeth bright as moon seeds
Even against the dust
The broken lull
Of a world made
Weary by its scrolling storms
Is it 500 you say
And how many kids
Did we lose today
As if ratios rank all
Measure of character
For the distant audience
Twittering pentameter
Sonnets slung from trees
Like faded photos
A crowd scene craned for poets
In boots and fatigues
Who are the nameless
Revolutionaries now united
By maternal affection
They ride the Orontes and Zambezi
On the backs of requiem sharks
Far from the Rio Desaguadero
Way up the Mississippi
From the Rockies
We flow down
To the Rio Grande
Trace the shape
That defines another
Borderland between
The impossible sum
Of here and home

A MOST PERFECT ASSIGNMENT

I cannot proceed in the usual way
Enumeration of sea arm, river mouth, headland

The common mass will not conjugate
Its path of old resistance

Rip tides carry caution
To the crooked smile of the sun

We will tack into this windward sound
Dividing by odd numbers

Each dot an expiation
Each dash a sigh

A code of courteous subtraction
The false promise of silent protest

Backwards we count
Up a paper ladder

Stick pins in the map
To prick recall

A letting of the past
Pooled history

Discoveries dragged or danced
In a manner not ours alone

Along the underbrush
Cracks in the foliage

Other selves struck down
Immemorial indivisible facts

Nodding they too raged
Fought where you fell

Sought another to fool the masses
Or build their splendid monuments

Did your family find you kindly
What of other mounted sufferings

Beyond this emphatic clutter
Of earthly paradise

Where did you find yourself
When it was most difficult

Did you dip precisely between
Other bodies of water

Bordered by shivering skin
Knee-deep in a glacial lake

On fourteen-hundred feet
Of mountainous forgetting

Did you attest to the ants below
Bustling or bombing

Or holding someone's ground
Another clever invention

Branded by the same words
For what gets taken away

Where the air grows thin
Blue bells sway

Against a ridge of dominant trees
Oblivious to their carpet of caress

DRAMATIC VERBAL SITUATIONAL
Washington, DC
July 4, 2019

Tanks on flatbeds roll through
Flaunting bygone dread
To junk-fed masses cheering
We have elected to be
Dumbly undisturbed
By division on parade

Is there another leading poll to stop
Our dark departing manifest entropy
Our pledge of convenience
To greenback allegiance
Protecting the wrong kinds of rights
A gross domestic malfeasance

Wastelands where metal's more
Welcome than children
Behind steel bars before chrome barrels
Bound by contracts ironclad
We shout for release as we look at our screens
But cannot make a sound

Here in the city of poets
An obtuse fog
Pulls our murals down
It's a sorry stage this concealing
Old outrage with more unhealing
To belie what our forefathers did

But by jingo we do shake our fists
At frail canaries in our midst
Hope the oil and coal beds thrive
Ignore the Appalachian addict child
Who climbs the ridge to poach the prize
Of his grandpa's ancient ginseng root

He'll pawn the healing cure
For cash enough to buy more pain
From the patron of the museum
Who peddles the pills
That make him sick
But fund more art

So I bury my poem
Beneath this tree
Quietly chopping

HERO'S JOURNEY
For Emilio Villalba

Of twin trees and trailing Sunday smoke
Of yellow sand on mortal ash cans etched
Spidery grids bear the thrust of bottled centuries
Skulls that inch like long-considered lies
Shaped as self-portraiture mirrored
Before porcelain women whispering
Up high hung walls
Tied to the tales of despots
With their lingering eyes
Leapt glossy from the goat mask
Mesmerized by surrender...
You have delivered this falcon
His beak of broken code
Sealed his lips of lapis plate
With the omen of worldly success
Vowing this is the work of scarabs
All paths fold into this our age
Drawn by screaming horses
Towards your giant footprints

POSTSCRIPT

I am one
Body of water
Altogether
Open ocean
Loose lake over
Man-made cave
Connoting grace
But beneath not
Tame never resting
Or fully fathomable
Being so surcharged
Carrying all this alluvial life
Island chains & hotspots
To transform fault and boundless core
Hearts of shifting permission

II.

Convergent Boundaries

THE SOUND OF MELTING

It is dangerous to say heart
Each letter a feathered vane
Arrowed infinite & full
Of all the time we've run down
The seas nearly drowned
From so much endless need
To own beyond ourselves
Could we not dip-slip
Beneath the curtain
Buoy the liquid light
Far from our hot &
Greedy hands

STILL OF THE SKY SMILE

In the naked tooth of the day
Looming and similar shapes
Mock the general order
We are more and less alone
Bones circled by dust
Thoughts darting through

Or would you stop to consider
What we could lose
And hold on
To this fractional end
Bowed to a towering moment
Set upon our larger plate

Shy howl
To a widening sky
According no nation
No wiser than degrees
No halo rounder
Breathing this air

POEM IN EXCHANGE

for my ferocious
every day madness
i pen a morning glory
to remind me i should
wake up tomorrow
to the hard material work
of desire's totalizing release
flush with
the situational / slash imagined
"experience" elevated
by erotical quotation marks

I ONCE LOVED A POEM

Child of the deep song
Loose-footed fretting
Our nights of sweet disorder
Mischief under pagan moons
The words we stole
As from the gods we hid
Behind knees and wrists
Spellbound but demure
Madness there was
To our stanzas
Only we could hear
The breaking of souls
Bored by easy rhythm
Wooed by the pretty
Seaweed slyly seeping
Laughter through the wall
The fleeting pleasures
We have whispered to others
To take their sounding
Inside me I feel you rise
Standing as I bind my legs
Behind your back wrap
Trembling tenderly arms
Towards this beastly beauty

& MOST
12/12/2019

My first unwrapping
Of the gifts you part so freely with
Taste of time and how to hold
Loosely and more dear
The dueling art
Of lull and letting go
I roll their pure antiquity
Cool as a wish across my palm
Worn green stones that survive
Their hawkish times
Ruled by hard river openings
And harder men
But these beads are carved
More by comity
Than tricks of trade or suasion
Strung to a softer strength neither
The impatience of staccato nor
Dazzle of a forking blaze
For among varietals of cloud
To ground lightning are a type
Most rare of linked and longer duration

FIND ME IN FRAGMENTS, CANTOS

It was my turn
to be less abrupt
loose with the outward
motion-making. Lean

ideas opened by brash
flourish. First signs
vertically down-sent
storm-like in pursuit

the shape of desire
stutters speech. Ergo
spike oil many trouble
the ordinary angle.

You don't say lavender
if you want cloud
rain is never gentle.

Lain we long ways
in the battered grass
notions of spears
bent at random shadows

subterranean sounds
seek an invisible speed
what we take as flat line
ladders the silence. Roots

horizontal, it's how you reach
the blue-violet pitch.
Hesitation edits the length
magic lanterns make. Go,

curve without end.
Beginnings made
the dalliance of corners
infinite catastrophes

cherished dross. Doubtless
said many times before but not

for nothing as nothing
need break the sun's fall

ANNIVERSARY POEM

For Matt Gonzalez

You are not formed as the diamond
From a single element and known
To be transparent, nor like an emerald
Lushly moody and prone to break

More to the fiery luxury of a ruby offering
Defense in battle or invention when blue
Sapphire you set asterism to the page as
Long-rayed lines, glittering word-gems

I glide through their agile beauty
Unhandled as a much-loved cup
Earthy clay and pale tracings
Taste roused for another day

Listening for bird song
Making a nest of my body

DON'T BEND ON THIS

I've been wrestling with a villanelle to unriddle the phrase that appeared in your hallway today. I'm not sure why I thought a formal French frame could help decode words scratched in black marker across exposed drywall. Common words in common space. Connotations unknown. Perhaps the work of a laborer. Or neighbor. Also unknown.

I've played with the key lines in the opening tercet. Explored rhymes for *this* – miss, kiss, dismiss, bliss, abyss, reminisce. Chasing meaning in patterns that transcend a now lost intention. People search for certainty. The provocations of the word *wall* – all, crawl, sprawl, brawl, haul, fall – are similarly dangerous. The brain is trained for cycles.

Swinging doors. Thoughts opening. Thoughts closing.

The fixed poetic form proves too rigid. Naturally. It's forcing a quest not my own. A buttoned-up scheme someone more skilled might master but I wish – just for this moment – to breathe into this koan. Invite it to breathe into me. A glimpse of non-duality.

Yet this still signifies otherness. Might I sign less?

Palms know the gesture of less. Movement across canvas, through water. Skin at the edge. Wing, fur, rock, scale, bone.

Beyond what expands without opening or closing.

No symbol

Or warning

Momentary

Just

Don't Bend on This

UPON HEARING A RECORDING
At the Exploratorium

I am listening to Muriel Rukeyser
Conjugating water into wine
À la paramecia amid the pop and hiss
Of other poetical scientists
Something about cilia-surrounded horns
Makes me strain for Bunk Johnson
See I'd spit teeth to learn the trumpet
Or meet the high priestess of soul
Who would never surrender the sound of her own
Ache to feel less alone
Secure in her lady slipper self
Never forcing the choice
Between waiting or running
Or acting like you've won
Like President Eileen Myles
In her White House without homelessness
A poet in every pot
Not wandering lonely or mild
She raised a platform for two women loving
A female face to grace a greenback
But hey I have wives too
More money than currency
And a sterling child
Who gives thanks for winter
Doesn't need a metonym
Or stand in religion
For certain people
Certainly those certain people
You miss even as you meet them
Wishing you could never leave and keep on
Loving nonetheless
Your card said manifest
A there-there as Gertrude Stein observed
The language we all speak
Repeats but did you
Mean it when you said the words

You'd give up
Oysters just for me
A ritual to be now and new
Happy on this stage in realization
Color is nothing but a confusion of light
Glory to be book-drunk people-drunk
& pulsing with oblique destiny
Your card said forgiveness
One atom dispersed and another split open
A social algorithm solved
That can't be sold
Or blown by mere
Molecular embouchure
Slang formed notes
Pulled apart in segments
A peel of hot brass
Citrus bright
Nostalgia for tomorrow-
Tomorrow
I am so-so
Grateful for this life

WERE THE EYE NOT SUN-LIKE
In memory of Anne Dunlap

I end another week in avenues that stretch to sunset. A routine of
small devotions. I will keep loving. This town, this life, this
moment.

Some tasks are effortless. But it's useful to set intentions.
Awareness is additive. Exponentially. I recognize that I brighten
in the contours of sound and color; yet falter in the rigor of detail.

I'll say: Here is a translucent tunnel. The journey to arrive will not
be described. You are dropped in. I will whisper unmakable. Will
you go? The repetition of a word like deeper can cause an
instinctive rush. The tongue is a tuning fork. Beneath the skin.
Conductivity.

These are things you know because your earth-body is electric.
How to bend at the knees and open your chest. That the shoulder
closest to the wave is everything. Fate being one muscle. You
must get square with fear.

Things your water-body knows. We become what we lose. We
must yield what we grow. The heart is a tide pool. Hi and low.
Look from the shore to the flower to the star, then back again.

People mold people. Exponentially. My friend Ben married Anne
55 years ago. Theirs was a rare excitement. In Greece, we rode the
ferry from Piraeus to Hydra together. Her laughter an unsinkable
sun.

Johann Sebastian Bach composed six works for solo violin shortly
after the death of his wife. His cryptic title Sei Solo sounds like
"six solos" but translates as "you are alone." His Chaconne for D-
minor belongs to the final movement of the second partita. From
within the lament of a descending chromatic bass begin the double
stops. Two strings played at once. The sound is not love. It is the
memory of love.

Stars carry their own memories. The light of past incandescence. We need stars in our eyes to see them. What we call shooting stars aren't stars at all but the dustfall of meteors. Astral spindrift like the spray of a cresting wave.

It is wise to practice ways of falling. Sometimes you need use that shoulder to punch through and get clear. Arch like a rainbow that is really a sphere. Then go again.

The world is a tidepool. Shallow and rocky. In turns submerged and scorched. Battered by wind and prevailing current. I think barnacles and starfish are very brave. We have things to learn from their liminal bodies.

ABUNDANCE AND GOOD LUCK

For Jason Morris

Or could you look away
When the card is turned as if
It were not your own eyes fluttering

I know too few things about Chinese poetry
Where geese are favored and a descent to sand
Can mean a poet stranded in exile

From this I take courage
I shall not abandon the club-footed bird
I have written about for ten lines

Let this small passerine scroll
Towards an affirming symbol
Is it Art that's suggested

When one male of the species
Begins to woo by raking
1400 sounds a second

From his wings
This strain of small violins
So pleased the female manakins

His mutation has grounded generations
Their once-hollow bones reforged
To make flight impossible

Was it choice or mere preference
That evolved his legacy to declare
Let's be instruments of beauty

Blurs of auburn
Rattling low in the saddles
Of heavy-stemmed trees

Where water becomes air becoming water
Firecracker, rain stick, this night
Loose with your impossible vocabulary

CONSIDER TRANSITIONS

Two Figures
Merge
Yin soft
Yang bright
Over globe
Spills to pond
An undertow
Deeper than skin
Or spoken intention
Grown subtle by
Unfinished arrival

III.

Strike Slip

OMISSION OF HORIZON

Dark on a day just beyond that shift
To saving daylight
Everyone's more tired
Of these hills where it will not rain
Yet the mountains rage with fire again
A speaker on a polished screen says
Something other than what I hear
Staring at a grey line
Waking through still branches
What has never looked this way before
Feels sparse as light for me
The endless momentary
Van Gogh traveling by train
From Paris to Provence
Eyes wide for what's right in front
Wondering if he were in Japan
Among the flattening effects of the sun
Distilled to diagonal, nuance, and vivid flash
Cropped close up or as seen from the sky
Life's outline outliving its own detail
The world afloat
Bridges in the mist
Something that doesn't end

BUILT A PICTURE YESTERDAY

A man dragged a bag across the street
Shouted to a dissatisfied-looking woman
On a billboard who may or may not be aware
How she really feels is up to her and perhaps
They could have stayed friends — shared a bond
Introduced some years later say how funny we
Don't remember why the settling nothing
Is never far behind though this is not the point
My undertone was to be ultramarine
A story of ocean and sky exchanging glances
Finishing each other's sentences too shy to call it's
Magic how two things combine to make a new being
Teach a fresh lesson irremovable from the first
Sense for the series is the work
Not a single object to celebrate rather
The sum-verse of all the effort that's never seen
Mistake and retake — echo and remain —
Advancing no one perfect art as self
Has one central nerve to share the blood
The body does not count in days
Nor number its rhetoric
Winding hints along the way
A Latin meaning beyond the sea
A movement of celestial meter
The waves beat, the waves crash
Shortwave blue to violet sonnet
You a long-legged bird
Gliding the contour

ONE SYNONYM

It could be any time from early dawn
When the sidelong fog in silence nods
Across the brightening bay
Or later as the slow boats slip through
The last rays to dock just here
The canvas day remains
A sudden pagan mystery
Charcoal curves speak their lines
Asymmetrical eyes carved
To suggest surprise
One beryl sky lost to haze
Or mist loose and easy
There is more to this place
Neither ripe pears nor turning hips
Pepper mills shaped to diverge
The torso of a lone tower
Or two stems to share a glass
Yellow may bear witness
Stuttering in spills of scarlet red
Scenes of rest and return
Circle as they may
Within the small ambiguous picture
Reclined above a bedroom door
Promises kept in friendship
Gifts of glancing light
The giving to each indoor object
An outsized life
A revised hierarchy
Clouds in the sea
Bottles in the air
Endless repetitions
Of first encounters
Contrary landscapes
All these words

REPOUSSÉ AND CHASING
For Bob Hass and Brenda Hillman

He beat this maze
From bronze navel
To fruiting seed

She sang
In shells
And storms

Surfaced
Animals too
Nothing less

Epically to be
Undeflectable
As fragrant wood

Poems unbuttoning pearl by pearl
Underground moons in the eyes of trees
A white rooting real as sky as forest

GONSHI

For David Ligare and Gary Smith

I.

Wind pleats the valley
Unearths a sunken bell
Where it stirs we doze
In the dry grass hills gilded
Like a pride of lions
Chest-open limb-traverse
Tangled by the universal thirst
That links one to another

II.

Trees deciduous dust
The pasture's outer memory
Even so it will never be easy
To speak of this land's
Private overtures
Searched by scholars
For subtle aeons under
Stoney pulsation

III.

A glanced resemblance
Climbs the air
Asymmetrical against
The naked unshy moon
More gesture than form
As a shimmer on the ocean
Knows no color braver
Than this sheen

IV.
The secret suchness
Things as they alter
Thoughts that come home
Downy with wisdom
Unadorned as leaves
Or sandstone cliff
A why without answer
These are for the cows

ADAGIO CANTABILE

It's pouring down
I too am waiting
Less like rain
Than a lesson in rain
The earth demands
As a flower shouts
So little of what she wants
Listen for the leaves who've stayed
Loyal kin to the honey bee
Light industry in a minor scale
Each natural nervous development
Expands to please even the richly
Thick in our counterfeit bliss
Unhuddled
We are so
At the furrow
Of this loss
Strain for
The flicker
Of shadow rime
Our smallest symphony
A wind section
Bow at the chest
Just one movement
In the key of grace

UNCERTAINTY FACTOR

They'd been looking across the water
Towards some speck off the coast of Madeira
Decades later she'd find it again on a map
& discover she'd lost her bearings
For the mind is inclined to frame any sea as north
(our bodies pull like baby oceans towards the polestar)

But this slight volcanic isle sat to the south
Somewhere near the Canary islands
She pointed at the flat-topped rock
Knowing only a flightless species
Could call such desolation
Home

Why do some insects lose their wings
Ecology is never as simple as theory
Or the plans of humankind
A gene pool may be shallowed by wind
The beckoning of sea or indolent habit
Conceivably a stable habitat may be freely chosen

My father, who was seldom near
Proved flight muscles are incredibly costly
For insects to operate and maintain
My mother settled a thing or two about the living cell
Camouflage and organelle, the thinnest boundary of breath
But I didn't mean to speak of greater speciation

All around us are examples of Nature's rightness
If not exactness —
Memory is an organ of selection
She speaks in portals
I harmonium
Sequitur non sequitur

THAT GO-BETWEEN, THAT PRISM

For Lawrence Ferlinghetti

Blessed are beatitudes on the down beat
Blessed are thee who BYOB

Blessed are those who attend to landscapes
Of the living and the dying — much has been recorded

Of the still life —I must return and learn anew
As with any self-sprung tune

As with each fresh fact retold
One must hear it precisely again over & over

Several times before it can be known
And repeated amid the din

Of dire but aloof admonitions
The world's been crying out

Do you enjoy your own mind?
Who are we now?

Alone together
In another bygone world

I want the word *novel* back
I want each of you back

Racing down these hills
Towards what is not lost

Blessed be the new routine
Steeling the coalface

I am not waiting
You are not waiting

The sea, the sea
Up from the ash bed

Sweet mother sometimes
Dream crimson like fire

TEMPO RUMBATO

Arrows in chalk come up on sidewalks
Fern Pine, Peppermint Willow, Bay Fig
Blackwood acacia, Bracelet Honey Myrtle
Hedge Maple, River Wattle
Incense Cedar, Spanish Chestnut
6 Blue Gum Eucalyptus
Planted by a former slave
At yet another terminus of stolen time

Let us go
Night ninja day fairy
Gardens press their infinite variety
Moments more or less misplace themselves
For are we wicked quick or carelessly slow
Set against the green world of pure phrasing
Knee root and canopy
Sap rise and signal memory

Let's make this our harvest of surrender
Metal city meet wood pile
Dig with your dirt soft oar
Ancient networks run underground
Maps of filament corridor
Curvy mycorrhizal hills
Ants transiting arabesques more complex
Than any artificial thought can plot or seed

The fungi feed on withered leaves
Then favor back to nourish trees
Which we name for each other
Also to feel more
Fully human
Soliloquies of
Breech and progress
Nailed upon a cloud

INDIRECT OBJECT

Their preying eyes fix a loop with three pins
It took a few contrivances to knit this assemblage
Masquerade model of the known nature of things

They had worked to polish the mystery
Practiced breathing until the cold air
Made them strong enough to fly away

Then confessed
I am the bullfighter
The heart of the bull

Sister of the red scarf thrown

DÉRIVE DE L'ESPRIT

She hums in the fur
Was naked animal
On legs reclined
Thus and thus made
More beautiful
After forest
After snow
A greenness in her
Eyes closed listening
For the sharp claw
On the high branch
Her bear
Heavy w/ apples
Knows this hunger

IV.

Oblique Faults

FIRST ANALOGY

Redemption awaits
Its appointed day
Riles my solitary distractions

For just beyond this mortgaged door
Cardboard conquistadors
Fringe their sidewalk citadels

Another demonstration
Of what we've long known
This is not the deliverance

We imagined in offering
Green feather for leaden ore
Our beaks stood so open

In those days before when as fallen
Folk we broke the silent bars
Of sky with outstretched notes

And from our claws choked
The miracle like a rusted lamp
Swallowed by a hollow wish

White noise lapping
Galaxy is to universe
As knuckle bone is to regret

We, I have sealed a mountain of apology
Buried it in a box under so many slow dances
On the hard frost beneath our infinite sun

Which one day too will die yet moves me
Like a shoulder through the mineral grief
Of stone as a chorus of earth-shadows rise

There is an exorcism to awkwardness
An artifice bold as a flame tree or more
Bell blaze brown and scarlet bare to the branch

Fully free of leaf
And the undivided sweet
Fruit of its own season

ENVOI

The *they* of rough and ready opinion
Say a second bite from the same apple
Won't taste any better and only in fact
Brings one closer to the bitter core
How I miss my old lover's insatiable hands
This mouth moves easily to offers of regret

I wonder who else sees the harm of Nature
Forgetting the fiction of human dominion
Is this not what the pattern demands
You will bore of my battles
As I squander another 59 lines on a metaphor
Only to obscure the naked necessary fact

I want to emerge
Different than before
As if this world were the last apple
And this moment our lost garden
The only one we'll ever seek
& in which we may not hide

Hypnotized by the music of greed
Dumb to innuendo of glacial retreat
Vines curled back upon their own roots
Anxious to latch the gate safely
On the 12-thousand self-cannibalizing mollusks
Once used to dye the hem of a single gown
.
.
.
.
.
.

I hide behind visible layers of habitation
Choosing my words
Blossoms of terrible beauty

FUGITIVE COLOR

Sequestered I gather
The visible objects and angles
Of my days as they turn voiceless
Corners grown in drama and I make peace

With vagaries like a thin supply of lake pigment
The kind known to fade or go dark with time
I paint twilight in the mornings and the red memory
Of flesh made anxious by my shy approach

I set about to reconstruct the wall of my living
Room across a single sheet of cold pressed cotton
On the reverse side a spirit sketch -- my pepper tree
Dips her jasmine skirt to *passiflora's* lavish mop and arching
antlers

On a good day I soldier on with the still life ripe and raw
Plum, clay cup, an empty wine bottle's full-throated embrace
Of flamed admission & I will vow to play in this moment
Songs of radical tempo shift and going all the way

My path walks its wanderer scattering cinnamon
Landscape grown thick with scarlet leafwing
A father's ghost throws a net to his barefoot child
But her hands are full with firefly

Forest echo / Alizarin crimson

AND ALL YOU TOUCH AND ALL YOU SEE

On the wild edge of adolescence we toss
Cherry sticks to test our uppermost branches
Stretch mouths to measure the breath
And bounce of rain bolts
Taste heartbeats between the tracks
Mesh with the velvet vault of night

I can suggest but not assure if
The souls of sun-stars reassemble
Like white light through a prism yet
It's true that I saw the rainbow ray out
& that no hope I'd held until then
(Or since) seemed closer than your lips

For how many decades
Now beneath the icy sheets
A sleepless glacier is tucked back in
To its nest of underwater sky as the child
That I was will watch the one I have become
Seal her wishes in a jar by the door

I dream of my mother exotic in her lab coat
Freeze fracturing cells to map the interface
Where air-rich blood and the tissue of the lung elide
She finds them mirrored in the surface of the earth
Ribosomal clusters resembling African river deltas
The delicate lace of breath as a drift of Siberian snow

Seen from space
We are all rift and healing
Listen long enough
To the *Dark Side of the Moon*
Somehow everything opens
A tall jar of sighs

LITTLE SHIPS AT THE NARROWEST PART

Spindrift unsigned
Sand & wave wind

Whips chalk from white cliffs
Draws long tear trails

Along this rented window pane
A cadre of history has arrived

Sadness settled in to séance
From a bluing beyond all birds

The trees will never forget
Cloaked in calm demeanor

They warn the flowers
Not to grow petulant

Or cold to the dawn
Go seek the soul at work

Like an underground foundry
Like a fault trembling

An ache beneath
The sea's evasion

Known to marine methusalehs
Who bed her briny mystery

Send embassies of morning
Felicity of flint fossil

Ultraviolet tidings of salt
Hands dusted like wings

TALK ABOUT THE PASSION

what spent kingdoms will slip from me as I pass
through vague and cobwebbed shapes
to this final arch of uncut stone

I have desired wild heaven
a tame and blameless destiny
aspired to give such words a home

dream / wake /touch
the heart pumps & pumps
the earth pumps & pumps

an absolute happening
undraped to hipbone
driftwood / quicksand / footfall

the nude moon
the naked sun
edges of me

alter the choice

these hands feel
like the first fish
tumbling water

I know a forest so densely green
birdsong can't get through so the moss
weeps with the memory of lost music

below the skeletal echo of coral reefs
primitive shadows take up
their makeshift instruments

composing water into water

WINNOWING FAN

One wants the doves to return
I heard this from thunder

        Night leans as wine-dark days run long
        Rust is proof that metal is not immune

Perfume of sorrow nor parables of thorn
We must love our disordered angels

        Dawn to the shadow of obvious wings
        I am not your eagle

Know that we must quit our monsters
That bluff is flecked with golden apples

        Feral wolves and the motives of moths
        You will miss this soft wash of disorder

The persistence of touch
Disturbance of downtrodden grass

        The body-body must choose
        Olive tree or the miracle of rivers

Trembling before your island home
Command your wind in delirious spindles

        Understand before you leave
        The sea knows nothing of the sea

RITES OF SPRING

Have I looked back at loveliness and sighed
Edna St. Vincent Millay

gangly species of crane
rufous about the neck
trumpets fidelity needs
no fingers for his song

i type and grasp about
my nest a lone caress
language lain in darkness
warm and worn for only

my heart too replies with
fallen stars and broken shells
a cry of compound communion
a latent action laddered

like the chain of light climbed
to reach the next strike line
august at the bridge
antigone to the end of the ocean

ALLUVIUM

Doctors in the low-lying netherlands
spot a secret wellspring lurks in the nook
where nasal cavity meets throat. This would
be the first new anatomical find in centuries
which is a thrill for science but I question what
another organ has to teach me when of the three
glands I already know the one below my tongue
is hardly in sympathy with time's parched desire.
Yet remember once it was civilized to clasp hands
after spitting on them as to seal a bond stronger
than one's own word and proof perhaps
the body is still capable of surprises

DISAPPEARING POET OF ALWAYS

A second chance ecology
Of random counting
                stick / stone / rock / bone

Prisoners chalk the days down
White pickets on rough gray wall

Not to forget
            <<pressure against the bank>>
Say Their Names*

The souls we never lose
Put language through the land

Quarry asks what is faster than a leaf can crawl?

                Single stem in a post-flowering state
(orphan was to wind rushed)
            the heart of a stag
            that of the earth

More than thought
Energy excavates &returns

Subject position is one cipher
For the solitude of unbridled gloom

Spirit insatiable this
The crux is   *remember*
all things good eventually are

Street lamps draped in red paper
Forefend fevers invisible to human ears

Even to the end reconsider
The syrinx, the dandelion clock

How much of your body
Is actually even you

OVERHEAD

I imagine myself
Call up a cloud regatta
Featherlike seeds in lieu
Of sails drift above, alone
I lean into the same circle
Ever so slightly widening my path
With each turn the wind turns too
Evening the footnotes
Islands of the makeshift mind
To the perfume of spices
I toss a ball of heart strings
Faraway, entirely
Thunder, ellipsis
Falls of dark matter
Only this misty outcrop of stars remains
I may declare them self-land
Will scoop their rising
As volatile value
A measure of tides
Endlessly replenishing
The original savanna
To all four corners of this dream
Here there will be no horizon
To seduce my undoing
Only delicate threads
In the full mirage
Of my alter sky

Tamsin Spencer Smith, 2018

Tamsin Spencer Smith is a poet, painter, novelist, and essayist. She's published two previous collections of poetry, *Word Cave* (RiskPress) and *Between First and Second Sleep* (FMSBW), and her verse appears in various anthologies and journals. Her first novel *XISLE, a novel* was released by FMSBW Press, as Number 3 in The Divers Collection. Her paintings have been widely exhibited in San Francisco, including at: Adobe Books Backroom Gallery, Modern Eden, The Luggage Store Gallery, Guerrero Gallery, Incline Gallery, and The Midway. Smith also writes art reviews and catalogue essays, the most recent of which, "A Summer Drawing Circle: The Story of Joan Brown's Mary Julia Series" was published by the George Adams Gallery in 2020.

Born in Cambridge, England, Tamsin now lives in San Francisco, California. She attended Kenyon College, where she graduated summa cum laude with highest honors in English. She is a Henry Crown Fellow at the Aspen Institute.

.

THE PAGE POETS SERIES

Number 1
Between First & Second Sleep by Tamsin Spencer Smith

Number 2
The Michaux Notebook by Micah Ballard

Number 3
Sketch of the Artist by Patrick James Dunagan

Number 4
Different Darknesses by Jason Morris

Number 5
Suspension of Mirrors by Mary Julia Klimenko

Number 6
The Rise & Fall of Johnny Volume by Garrett Caples

Number 7
Used with Permission by Charlie Pendergast

Number 8
Deconfliction by Katharine Harer

Number 9
Unlikely Saviors by Stan Stone

Number 10
Beauty Will Be Convulsive by Matt Gonzalez

Number 11
Displacement Geology by Tamsin Spencer Smith

www.ingramcontent.com/pod-product-compliance
Lightning Source LLC
Chambersburg PA
CBHW032053040426
42449CB00007B/1096